FACING THE UN...
CRISIS IN ...

UNDERCURRENTS Series Editor J.J. Lee

Facing the Unemployment Crisis in Ireland

KIERAN A. KENNEDY

CORK UNIVERSITY PRESS

First published in 1993 by
Cork University Press
University College
Cork
Ireland

© Kieran Kennedy 1993

British Library Cataloguing in Publication Date

A CIP catalogue record for this book is available from the British Library

ISBN 0 902561 67 7

Typeset in Ireland by Seton Music Graphics Ltd, Co. Cork
Printed in Ireland by ColourBooks, Baldoyle, Co. Dublin

CONTENTS

ACKNOWLEDGEMENTS

I want to thank Joe Lee for inviting me to write this pamphlet for the *Undercurrents* series and for his encouragement throughout the task. I am grateful to Sara Wilbourne of Cork University Press for her expert advice on presentation, and also to the other staff members of the Press for their courtesy and cooperation at all times. I would like to record my debt to the following who offered valuable comments on earlier drafts: Deirdre McHugh, National Economic and Social Council; Michael Casey, Central Bank of Ireland; Philip Lane, Harvard University; my ESRI colleagues, John Bradley, Bob O'Connor and Jerry Sexton; and Finola Kennedy. Special thanks are due to Florence O'Sullivan for her incomparable efficiency in typing my illegible scripts. Responsibility for the final product is mine alone.

Kieran A. Kennedy
April 1993

1. Introduction

In January 1993, for the first time ever registered unemployment in Ireland surpassed 300,000, or 21 per cent of the labour force. Ireland now has the unenviable distinction of topping the EC unemployment league table, with a rate nearly double that of the EC as a whole, when the rates are adjusted for comparability with each other.[1]

Everyone seems to agree that unemployment is Ireland's most serious economic and social problem. Yet the nation's span of concentration on the issue is brief and sporadic. In 1978, the then Taoiseach, Mr Jack Lynch, stated that his government did not deserve to be re-elected if it allowed the unemployment level to rise to 100,000. Yet by the mid-1980s we had accommodated ourselves to a level 2½ times higher. When unemployment stabilised and fell slightly in the second half of the 1980s, we breathed a collective sigh of relief and were not unduly disturbed by the fact that the main reason for the fall was the resumption of large scale emigration.

With the choking off of emigration outlets since the onset of depression in the United Kingdom and other economies from the beginning of 1991, there was a renewed flurry of attention to the unemployment situation, culminating in the establishment of the Culliton Review Group on Industrial Policy, the Task Force on Employment, and at a later stage the Oireachtas Committee on Employment. Public concern erupted further in August 1992 as a series of redundancy announcements threatened to bring the number on the Live Register to 300,000 and in response the government hastily assembled a package of £150 million funding for industry. Yet just over a month later, a march organised in Dublin on 6 October 1992 by the Irish National Organisation for the Unemployed attracted no more than 2,000 persons, and news coverage of the event was swamped by the announcement of the government's proposals on abortion.

It appears that public concern is actively engaged only by sharp increases in unemployment, and not by the underlying level, so that concern evaporates once a new plateau is reached, no matter how high that plateau may be. This is a significant impediment to developing an adequate response to the problem. The reality is that there may be little that can be done in the short term in the face of sudden sharp increases in unemployment, particularly those emanating from conditions abroad: indeed there is a danger that attempts to implement *ad hoc* solutions in the short term could make matters worse for the long-term. Our real concern should be to address the appallingly high underlying rate of unemployment, from which little relief can be expected even by the end of this decade on the basis of current prospects and policies.

In this paper I argue that any effective attempt to address the unemployment crisis in Ireland would require sustained effort over a long period, and that this effort would be painful for many established interests. While there are choices about the way the problem is approached, all of them have unattractive features, and none of them can provide a quick or certain solution. Such a line of argument is most unpalatable. Nevertheless, it represents no more than the plain truth, and the consequences of not confronting it now could be even more unpalatable later. If, therefore, the unemployment crisis is to be tackled effectively, there is an urgent need to mobilise and harness public concern in order to develop and sustain a sense of national purpose. It is my hope that this paper will contribute to that objective.

The paper is structured as follows. Given that job scarcity is not new in Ireland, it is important to provide a historical perspective, which is done in Section 2. The incidence and consequences of unemployment are summarised in Section 3, while Section 4 discusses causes. The scale of the future challenge facing Ireland is outlined in Section 5. Section 6 discusses the broad options that might be considered in attempting to bring about a major reduction in unemployment. The energetic pursuit of any of these options would require acceptance by the community at large of fundamental changes, and the question of how such changes might occur is considered in Section 7. Since it is not clear that radical changes will be accepted or implemented with sufficient vigour, Section 8 suggests some moderate reforms within the limits of what might be acceptable: such reforms would still leave us with high unemployment even at the end of this decade, but would enable us to enter the next decade in a more credible position to effect a greater impact. Concluding remarks are made in Section 9.

2. HISTORICAL RECORD

It is essential to stress that unemployment in Ireland is only one manifestation of a deeper and more pervasive problem, namely, that employment has never grown fast enough to absorb the potential increase in the labour force at the wage levels prevailing in Ireland. Over the full span of its history since Independence, the most unique feature about Ireland is that the level of employment is now about 10 per cent less than it was in the 1920s. No other country in the western world has had a similar experience.

The response to the inadequate rate of employment growth has been manifested in different ways at different times. Most of all it has shown up in massive emigration: since Independence net emigration has amounted to 1½ million persons. Even when emigration opportunities were limited, the full impact in earlier times (e.g. during the Great Depression in the 1930s) did not show up in the unemployment figures, but rather in the form of under-employment in agriculture and poverty in urban areas. Thus, in the twenty year period 1926–46 the decline in agricultural numbers was only 85,000 compared with nearly 200,000 in the subsequent fifteen year period 1946–61, and many who stayed on in the earlier period did so only because there was no other option. In more recent times, however, when emigration opportunities have been curtailed, the scarcity of jobs at home shows up primarily in higher unemployment – due to such factors as the increased urbanisation of the work force, the improvement in unemployment compensation both in absolute terms and relative to the UK, and the easing of the rules for registering as unemployed. The current unemployment crisis in Ireland, therefore, is not so much a new problem, as a new manifestation of a deeper problem that has been endemic in Irish history.

Taking the broad sweep since Independence, the weak jobs performance derives chiefly from Ireland's poor rate of economic development, which was the worst in Europe, apart from the United Kingdom. This experience has been extensively analysed in other studies (*see in particular* Kennedy et al. 1988 and Lee 1989). Ireland's progress in economic development, however, has not been uniformly bad, and there has been a substantial improvement in the rate of economic growth over the past thirty years compared with preceding history. Why, despite this improvement in growth, do we still have such a dismal jobs performance?

In fact, Ireland did experience some growth in employment over the last thirty years, and the level now is about 10 per cent higher than in 1960, whereas previously employment was falling. During the 1960s and up to the oil crisis of 1973, Ireland had positive employment growth though at a very low rate of about one-third of 1 per cent a year. This rate, however, was much the same for the EC as a whole. In fact if allowance is made for the much higher share of agriculture in Ireland – a sector in which employment was falling everywhere – the growth of non-agricultural employment in Ireland, at 1.8 per cent per annum from 1961 to 1973, was double the EC average. This gave reason to hope that once the weight of agriculture declined and industry and services became more dominant, the maintenance of higher growth in non-agricultural employment would soon lead to satisfactory overall increases in employment.

Although employment growth in Ireland in the sixties matched the growth in the EC, it was not sufficient to bring down unemployment in Ireland because of the higher potential increase in the labour force. Only with the aid of significant though falling emigration – a total of 170,000 left in the ten years 1961–70 – was it possible to keep unemployment stable at a rate of about 5–6 per cent. This level was much higher than in Europe generally, though not too much above that in the US, where unemployment was then typically higher than in Europe despite greater employment growth.

THE EXPERIENCE SINCE 1973

The year 1973, when the first oil crisis began, marks the advent of the new era of high unemployment in the western world. It would have been astonishing if Ireland had escaped, given its historic record of labour surplus, and the degree to which it is influenced by world developments. Yet, remarkably, the rise in unemployment in Ireland from 1973 to 1980 was less than in much of the rest of the western world (*see* Table 1), so that at the end of the 1970s Ireland's unemployment rate was roughly in line with the general picture in Europe and the US. Ireland's achievement was all the more remarkable given that the growth of its labour force in this period was unusually high – because of domestic demographic developments, mentioned below, and also the fact that migration had now reversed into a significant net inflow.

The relatively low rise in unemployment in Ireland over the period 1973–80 was associated with an unprecedented growth in employment during that period. Non-agricultural employment rose at an annual average rate of 2.2 per cent per annum from 1973 to 1980, almost matching the growth in the US and over

TABLE 1:

Unemployment Rates (%) in Ireland and other countries,
selected years since 1973

	1973	1980	1985	1990	1991	1992 (est.)
Ireland	5.7	7.3	17.0	13.4	14.9	16.1
UK	3.0	6.4	11.2	6.8	8.7	10.5
EC	2.9	6.4	10.8	8.4	8.7	9.6
US	4.8	7.0	7.1	5.4	6.6	7.3

Sources: OECD Economic Outlook, No. 52, December 1992, Table R.18 for
1973–91; Table 49 was used to estimate the figure for 1992 on a comparable
basis, except for the Irish figure which is based on ESRI Quarterly Economic
Commentary, Winter 1992/93. The unemployment rates are based on ILO/OECD
guidelines, and differ from the registered unemployment figures (see note 1, this
volume).

three times the growth in the EC. Unfortunately, the overall growth
in employment in Ireland in this period relied too much on increased
government borrowing at a rate which could not be sustained. In
particular, the programme launched by the new government in
the middle of 1977 to increase public expenditure and reduce
taxes in the interests of reducing unemployment was singularly ill-
judged, given that the exchequer borrowing requirement and the
balance of payments deficit were already at a high level when the
strategy was initiated. By the time the second oil crisis struck in
1979, these magnitudes had reached unsustainable levels and Ireland
was burdened with servicing a hugely expanded national debt.

In the course of the expansionary phase since 1960, indigenous
demographic factors changed in a way that exerted, and continues
to exert, a major influence on the growth of the potential labour
force. Over the twenty year period 1960–80, when the natural
increase in the EC population was falling from 8.0 to 2.7 per
1,000, the rate rose in Ireland from 9.9 to 12.2, and the rise in
the young active age groups was even greater. During the 1960s

the marriage rate rose and the age of marriage fell. Although fertility was also falling, the birth-rate remained high up to 1980. Given that the population was growing throughout this period, and very rapidly in the 1970s, this involved a rise in the annual number of births from a long-standing figure of about 60,000 to a peak of 74,000 in 1980. This substantial increase will continue to be reflected in a high potential inflow of labour force entrants up to the end of the century. Moreover, even though the Irish birth rate fell substantially in the 1980s, the rate of natural increase in population in Ireland remains above that of every other EC country.

Ireland was in a highly vulnerable situation in the face of the world depression following the second major oil price increase in 1979, and the first half of the 1980s was to prove one of the most painful phases in Irish economic experience since Independence. The volume of GNP was essentially stagnant, manufacturing employment fell by 38,000, building employment by 27,000 and the overall reduction in employment was nearly 80,000. While net emigration resumed again in 1980, the level remained low in the first half of the decade because of the adverse employ-ment situation in the UK. Unemployment was rising in most of the western world in this period, but the deterioration was much greater in Ireland. Indeed, as Table 1 shows, most of the phenomenally high rise in unemployment experienced by Ireland since 1973 has been concentrated in the first half of the 1980s, but that should not obscure the fact that the sources of this rise lie partly in the preceding period.

The considerable economic recovery in Ireland in the second half of the 1980s, which paralleled the recovery abroad, brought about some increase in employment and a reduction in unemployment. The reduction in unemployment, however, owed far more to resumption of high emigration than to employment growth. While employment rose by 47,000 from 1985 to 1990, emigration in that period amounted to 164,000. That the reduction in unemployment

7

was less than 50,000 (on a Labour Force Survey basis)[2] shows the impact of the continuing strong growth in the potential labour force. The renewed recession in the world economy in 1991 and 1992 gave rise to a double upward pressure on Irish unemployment. First, although the level of employment in Ireland did not fall – in itself a considerable achievement – it ceased to rise; and, second, rising unemployment abroad, particularly in the UK, deterred emigration so that the net outflow was negligible in 1991 and turned into a small net inflow in 1992.

PRODUCTIVITY AND INCOME

While the greatly enhanced growth in output over the last thirty years has brought some increase in employment, the increase has been much less than earlier experience would have promised. The corollary is that the growth of productivity (i.e. output per worker) has risen very strongly. Given full employment, rapid productivity growth would be very welcome as a means of raising living standards. Ireland remains much poorer than most member states of the EC, and a rapid rate of productivity growth is a necessary, though not a sufficient, condition of achieving a convergence in average income per capita (i.e. per head of population) towards EC levels. Unfortunately, Ireland has been much more successful in raising its productivity than in raising its living standards. There are two main reasons for this and they can be explained best by reference to Table 2, which shows the trend in three relevant variables in Ireland compared with the EC from 1973 to 1990.

The first of the variables in Table 2 is GDP per worker, which is a measure of labour productivity. Taking this measure at face value, Ireland has made striking progress since 1973 in reducing the productivity gap with the EC, which is now little more than 10 per cent. However, the growth of GDP in Ireland since 1973 depended heavily on government foreign borrowing and on inward

TABLE 2:

Productivity and income per capita in Ireland relative to the
European Community (EC 12 = 100)

	1973	1990
GDP per worker	69	89
GNP per worker	69	80
GNP per head of population	59	62

Sources: EC *Annual Economic Report 1991/92* and OECD *Labour Force Statistics*, 1970–90.

Note: GNP (gross national product) is the sum of GDP (gross domestic product) and net income outflows to the rest of the world.

foreign investment. Both of these gave rise to huge offsetting income outflows in the form of interest payments on foreign debt and profit repatriations by foreign multinationals. These outflows have substantially reduced the impact on domestic income of higher GDP. For that reason GNP, which takes account of the income outflows, is a truer measure of the income impact in Ireland. As may be seen from Table 2, the degree of convergence in GNP per worker towards the EC level is more muted than in GDP per worker.

Nevertheless, income per worker in Ireland has been catching up to some degree with EC levels, but this has not translated into a convergence in living standards for the population as a whole. As Table 2 shows, the gap in GNP per capita between Ireland and the EC is much wider than in GNP per worker and it has converged only slightly since Ireland joined the EC: in fact it is no closer now than it was in 1960. The reason is the relatively small and declining proportion of the population at work in Ireland, which is now the lowest in the EC at 31 per cent. The employment ratio is influenced by demographic factors, and to some degree Ireland's low ratio reflects social choices in favour of higher fertility and more spouses remaining on home duties. The major explanation of the low employment ratio, however, lies not in individual preferences but in the poor labour market conditions, manifest particularly in the high unemployment rate but also in a low rate of participation in the labour force and an age structure distorted by emigration. The low employment ratio means, for example, that in Ireland every ten workers have to support, on average, twenty-two dependants (defining as dependants all who are not in gainful employment), whereas in Denmark at the other extreme, every ten workers have to support only nine dependants.[3]

It is clear, therefore, that Ireland's relative poverty in an EC context is related to its inadequate employment performance. Moreover, it is highly unlikely that in the future Ireland could converge to EC income levels for its population as long as it carries such a high level of unemployment and associated dependency.

SUMMING-UP

Ireland's historically weak employment performance is closely bound up with long-standing inadequacies in its rate and pattern of economic development. Never for any sustained period did it create enough jobs to absorb the potential increase in the labour force, so that it has always had a problem of labour surplus even when full employment was the norm elsewhere. Traditionally this surplus was relieved chiefly through emigration, so that recorded unemployment, while high relative to other countries, never for long remained at crisis levels until the last twenty years – though undoubtedly there were at times higher levels of unemployment and underemployment that went unrecorded.

The huge rise in unemployment over the past twenty years arises not because the employment performance has notably deteriorated. On the contrary, despite the sharp fall in the first half of the 1980s, the employment level is still 60,000 above the 1973 level whereas up to the 1960s the long-term trend was downwards. Net emigration, however, has been greatly reduced, partly because of the general rise in unemployment worldwide and particularly in the UK. In the twenty years 1973–92 net emigration totalled 115,000 compared with about 400,000 in the preceding twenty years. There is, therefore, no great mystery in an arithmetic sense as to why 300,000 are now registered as unemployed. We are left with the deeper mystery, however, as to why the persistent labour surplus did not generate greater pressures for its solution.

3. INCIDENCE AND CONSEQUENCES

Who are the unemployed? Unemployment is far from being a random phenomenon, and not everyone is equally vulnerable. Even with a rate near 20 per cent and a good deal of movement into and out of unemployment, the majority of people do not experience unemployment and probably do not even see themselves as vulnerable. In a nationwide household survey conducted by the ESRI in 1987, respondents were asked how many years they had spent in employment and in unemployment since leaving full-time education. In the sample, 10 per cent of the adults were found to be currently unemployed, or 17 per cent of those adults currently in the labour force, but only 28 per cent of all the adults had experienced unemployment at any time during their careers.

At household level, it is true that few parents are now free from worry about jobs for their children, but nevertheless the majority of households remain immune from any direct contact with unemployment. In the survey referred to above, 38 per cent of households contained at least one household member who had experienced unemployment at some period, but this still leaves 62 per cent of households, none of whose members had ever experienced unemployment. In such circumstances, it is not surprising that a general concern about unemployment and the unemployed is so easily outweighed by particular concern about matters more directly affecting the majority of households – such as pay, taxes and mortgage interest. As we shall show, unemployment disproportionately affects those who are already less privileged – financially, socially, and educationally. If that position were reversed, and the more privileged were the ones most at risk of unemployment, who can doubt but that more would be done to address the problem?

Studies have shown that unemployment is always well above average for the unskilled and semi-skilled workers, in the industries (such as building) where such workers predominate, and in the localities in which they live. Hence the concentration of unemployment black spots – such as Tallaght, in some parts of which well over half the labour force is unemployed. Research at the ESRI has found a strong inverse relationship between educational qualifications and unemployment. The unemployment rate in 1988 among a sample of young females who had left post-primary school in 1982 without any qualifications was 50 per cent compared with a rate of 11 per cent for those who had sat the Leaving Certificate or higher examination: for males, the figures were 37 per cent and 12 per cent, respectively. The research also showed that the relative disadvantage faced by the unqualified on leaving school widened in the first 2–3 years after leaving school (Breen 1991).

Young adults under 25 tend to experience a higher-than-average rate of unemployment in all countries, due to age-related structural problems (lack of skills and experience) and frictional elements involved in settling into steady employment. In Ireland, as in most European countries, youth unemployment is higher than adult unemployment, and although the gap is no wider in Ireland, we still have exceptionally high youth unemployment because our adult rate is so high. In the middle of 1992, youth unemployment in Ireland was 27 per cent, compared with 18 per cent for the EC as a whole, and exceeded only by Spain and Italy where the rates were slightly above 30 per cent.

A particularly worrying feature of Irish unemployment is the number who experience long-term unemployment. Of the total of 280,000 on the Live Register at April 1992, close to 170,000 had been continuously on the register for over six months, and of these, nearly 120,000 had been unemployed for more than one year. This pattern is similar to the general experience of the EC but is not typical of the US or some of the Scandinavian countries, like Sweden and Norway, in all of which long-term unemployment is less than 10 per cent. Given that the likelihood of re-employment falls with the length of time spent unemployed, there is a danger in Ireland of creating a growing pool of permanently unemployed persons. Moreover, since these persons become disengaged from the organised wage bargaining process, the fact of their remaining unemployed imposes little or no moderation on pay claims; and they have neither the resources nor the skills to enable them to emigrate with confidence. These are some of the factors giving rise to the phenomenon known as hysteresis, the situation where a rise in unemployment may perpetuate itself.

It should be stressed that, though useful, knowledge of the incidence of unemployment, and of the characteristics of the unemployed, does not in itself provide a clear pointer towards solutions. For example, it does not at all follow, as some imagine, that, because the unemployed have low qualifications and skills, providing them with education and training will solve the unemployment problem. It is quite true that a country's potential for economic development depends greatly on the technological sophistication of its work force and the general level of labour skills. Upgrading these skills can create new areas of competitive advantage which should increase job opportunities in the long run. The process takes time, however, and many other steps are also required if more jobs are to follow. In the meantime, until job opportunities expand, the effect would be to redistribute unemployment rather than lower it. Redistributing unemployment would be a good thing if it alleviated the plight of those groups – such as early school-leavers or the long-term unemployed – suffering from extreme labour market disadvantage. But training alone may not redistribute unemployment in this way unless it is linked to measures to ensure that the trainees find a job on completion of training: otherwise, in a static labour market, those already better educated and trained compete even for lower level jobs, resulting in an inflation of the qualifications required for any available job and continuing to shut out the more vulnerable groups. None of this is to decry the importance of education and training, only to point out that it does not on its own provide a panacea.

COSTS OF UNEMPLOYMENT

Counting the costs of unemployment raises complex issues and does not always yield clear-cut answers. It is usual to approach the issue from three different perspectives – the unemployed themselves, the government and the country as a whole. As regards the unemployed, empirical studies show that, contrary to the view sometimes expressed, the majority of the unemployed incur a severe reduction in disposable income vis-a-vis earnings from previous employment. Of course there will always be abuses of the unemployment compensation system, as there are of all systems, but the image of the unemployed arriving in a Mercedes to collect dole payments is sheer fantasy.

ESRI research has demonstrated the strong link between poverty and unemployment. The poverty rate was found to be low in households where the head was an employee, whereas three in every five households where the head was unemployed fell below the poverty line (Callan et al. 1989). The research also showed that the huge rise in unemployment in the 1980s has pushed up the total numbers in poverty and greatly increased the share of the unemployed among those who are poor. These findings obviously have major implications for poverty policy: if one really wants to tackle poverty, then reducing unemployment should be the first priority. The adverse consequences for the unemployed are not confined to financial deprivation: the unemployed are also more vulnerable to social and psychological problems. Another study, for instance, found that the unemployed are five times more likely to suffer psychological distress than employees (Whelan et al. 1991).

Turning to the impact on government, public finances are seriously affected by unemployment both through the exchequer cost of paying unemployment compensation and related social benefits and through the loss of tax revenue. In 1992, the Estimates provision for unemployment compensation was £927 million. This does not represent a loss of revenue to the society as a whole but it does involve a transfer from taxpayers to the unemployed. If we relate the figure to the total number at work, it amounts to an average of over £15 a week per person at work. In addition, unemployment adds to the cost of public expenditure under a variety of other heads in the social welfare, health, housing and education areas. These are difficult to quantify, but are undoubtedly substantial. Thus, while there is much frustration among the employed population in Ireland about what are seen as penal tax rates, the reality is that no civilised country can expect to have low tax rates as long as one-fifth of the labour force is unemployed and has to be supported by taxpayers.

At societal level, the most obvious cost is the loss of goods and services which would have been produced by the unemployed if they had a job. In addition, there are resource costs arising from adverse social effects, such as vandalism, that may be partly caused by unemployment. A more fundamental, though less obvious, cost is the damage to the moral legitimacy of a society that tolerates 'human set aside' on such a vast scale. From a religious perspective, Pope John Paul II does not mince his words in the encyclical *Laborem Exercens* (1981) in stating that unemployment 'in all cases is an evil'. But from a humanist perspective also, participation is the essence of citizenship in a liberal democracy, and one of the most basic forms of economic participation is access to work – so that the denial of this form of participation to such a large minority constitutes a grave injustice. If the high level of unemployment were a passing phenomenon, then its implications would be less severe. But its persistence could create an enduring dualism in the economy and society, with an increasing minority left further behind in terms of access to jobs, income and education, and the attendant risk of similar deprivation being transmitted intergenerationally to the children of this marginalised section.

Why, then, in the light of such substantial costs is more not done to address the problem? An important part of the answer to this question is that reducing unemployment is itself not a costless process: if there were a painless way to cure unemployment it would have been implemented long ago. As we shall show later, measures likely to have a substantial impact in reducing unemployment would impose major costs on many important interests in society, the measures would take time to work and there is no absolute assurance that they would attain their goal. In these circumstances, the established interests in society in effect make the judgement that the costs of trying to tackle unemployment in a radical way would be more painful than the persistence of high unemployment. A worrying factor about that type of implicit judgement is that, because of the absence of any framework of long-term thinking, the ultimate costs of unemployment may not be adequately weighed up, especially given that the immediate costs are disproportionately borne by the weakest sections of society.

4. CAUSES

In considering solutions to any problem it is helpful – some would say essential – to have a clear knowledge of its causes. The question 'Why is unemployment so high in Ireland?' might seem to the layperson to be a straightforward question to which experts should by now be able to give a straightforward answer. It may come as a surprise to the layperson that there is as much disagreement among experts as there is among the general public on the answers to that question. Ireland is no worse off in this regard, however, than the rest of the world. A review article by a leading US expert on unemployment (Phelps 1992) of a major recent book analysing unemployment in OECD countries since the mid-1950s (Layard et al. 1991) concluded that 'there are not many findings in this volume that I am persuaded by, so far' and that in order to produce agreed findings 'it looks to me like a decade's work ahead of us'.

Why is there no unanimity about the causes of unemployment? A modern economy is a highly complex, dynamic mechanism in a constant state of flux. There are numerous interactions and feedbacks between key variables which make it difficult to distinguish cause and effect with any certainty: for example, a widening tax wedge may cause unemployment, but rising unemployment can also lead to a widening tax wedge. The variable we wish to explain, unemployment, may itself be only one manifestation of a deeper malaise – as was suggested earlier in the case of Ireland. Conflict of interest is inherent in economic life, and no group will readily accept an explanation counter to its own interest. The social sciences themselves are far from value free. On the contrary, most theories are value laden and different theorists have different values, of which they are not always conscious. Institutionalised boundaries between different social science disciplines can also be a limitation: economic phenomena may be determined by non-economic forces, yet some economists regard an understanding of the latter forces as outside their domain. Finally, as O'Donnell (1992) has argued, causal relationships in the economy and society identified through social science research necessarily remain tentative and incomplete – unless and until the ideas are tested in action to achieve economic and social goals.

The fact that we do not have an agreed analysis of the causes of unemployment in Ireland should not be taken as an excuse for inaction. Indeed, it is the rule rather than the exception that the formulation of economic strategies cannot wait until the ultimate explanations arrive – if they ever do – but must proceed on the basis of interim but, hopefully, intelligent judgements about the steps most likely to be beneficial. Nevertheless, some discussion of causes is necessary, if only to eliminate those clearly not in accord with the facts: it is extraordinary, for instance, how much attention has focused in Ireland on obstacles supposedly discouraging the unemployed from taking jobs that do not exist, and never have existed, in sufficient numbers.

One commentator has noted perceptively that 'a major error Ireland repeatedly makes is the assumption that the problems she faces are unique to her' (Wrigley 1985). Ireland is not in fact unique in having experienced a large rise in unemployment over the past twenty years: most of the western world also did. Given the generality of the malaise, it is reasonable to suppose that there must be large forces at work, which if not common to all countries, are at any rate universal in their impact. The Irish economy is exceptionally closely linked to the international economy, not only because of the high degree of external trade, labour mobility and foreign borrowing, but also because a big part of its industrial expansion has been based on foreign enterprise. It is important, therefore, to consider the major forces at work in the international economy in order to distinguish the degree to which the Irish experience differs.

WORLDWIDE UNEMPLOYMENT

The worldwide rise in unemployment followed a long period after World War II when the western world was so successful in combining full employment and steady output growth with a tolerable rate of inflation, that depressions had come to be regarded as obsolescent. Previously, the history of the capitalist system was one of recurrent depressions culminating in the Great Depression of the 1930s. The universal application of Keynesian ideas seemed to have banished this spectre. Keynes's essential message was that the overall labour market was not self-regulating: the economy did not automatically tend towards a full employment equilibrium, and the individual agents were powerless to bring this about. The state must intervene to ensure that the aggregate level of demand was sufficient to absorb the level of output capable of being produced at full employment. There were a variety of ways in which the state could so intervene, but, in practice, fiscal demand management policy came to be the favoured method.

With hindsight, it is possible to see more clearly that, during this phase of great prosperity, the world economy was changing – partly due to the success of the Keynesian prescription – in ways that made the prescription less effective. The first and most important change was the degree to which the world economy has become interdependent as a result of the freeing of trade and capital movements, increased travel and the radical improvements in communications. The Keynesian prescription was viable only in a closed economy, or in a world where the main countries were willing to act in concert. A policy of demand expansion by an open economy acting on its own would be bound to founder in the face of import leakages and balance of payments difficulties; and if no major country was willing to expand demand, while all sought to maintain employment by increased export competitiveness, the Keynesian dilemma of inadequate demand in the system as a whole would remain. Coping with this dilemma in a world of increasing economic interdependence called for enhanced international economic cooperation, which was not forthcoming.

The second major change in economic conditions has been the emergence of price inflation as a pervasive phenomenon of the postwar world. There is little doubt that the very success of the Keynesian solution underpinned inflation by removing the checks which had kept the general trend of prices stable in the UK, for example, over the previous two centuries – interspersed, of course, with periods of inflation and deflation. In a world in which full employment was assured, the restraints on wage pressures and on demands for public expenditure were greatly weakened – with inevitable consequences for inflation.

The third major qualification to the Keynesian prescription that emerged with experience was the need for a better balance between the level and the quality of demand stimuli. The Keynesian prescription suggested that in a depression *any* independent increase in demand through investment or government expenditure – even something as silly as digging holes and filling them in again – would boost the level of activity. While this may be true in the short term, it matters a great deal in the medium to long term how well the resources involved have been used. In practice, governments often failed to advert to the fact that wasteful investments and public expenditures, while giving a short-term boost, inevitably bring inflationary pressures in their train and ultimately damage employment prospects.

These cracks in the system were already showing up even before the first oil crisis in 1973, and inflation and unemployment were beginning to drift upwards in a number of countries. Nevertheless, the two oil price shocks greatly exacerbated the underlying structural problems. They represented a double blow in that they were both price inflationary and demand deflationary. They therefore produced at one and the same time rising prices, falling output, higher unemployment and large balance of payments deficits. In the response to the first oil price increase, many governments gave priority to offsetting the adverse effects on output and employment. Such action achieved only partial success and added the further problem of large public sector borrowing. The response of the major economies to the second oil price increase late in 1979 was very different. Fiscal and monetary policies became restrictive because of fears about the prospects for price inflation, balance of payments and public sector deficits. This approach was successful in bringing down inflation rates, but only at the cost of prolonging the depression and adding further to the already high unemployment levels.

The upheaval in the world economy was accompanied by a growing loss of faith by governments in their ability to intervene successfully to improve matters. This loss of faith was underpinned by the emergence, or re-emergence, of a dominant school of economic thought holding that such intervention is both ineffective and unnecessary. According to this view, the market economy, if only it is left to operate freely, is fundamentally self-regulating: unemployment would not persist if wages were sufficiently flexible. In the face of trade union intransigence, the government should not take responsibility on itself for maintaining full employment, since its actions would not only prove fruitless but would add to inflationary pressures. Such ideas gained influence in all western countries, even in those, like France, with a leftist government. Their credibility received a further boost from the collapse of the socialist systems in the USSR and East Europe.

With the renewed downturn in the world economy over the past two years, however, there are signs that the pendulum is swinging back again. This gives some prospect of a restoration of the essential Keynesian insight that markets cannot ensure an adequate and stable level of overall demand, while at the same time facing up to the problems that arose from the naive application of the Keynesian prescription. No one should underestimate the latter challenge, however. It must be admitted frankly that no one has yet devised a universal means of reconciling full employment and low inflation. With the growing economic power of major new players on the international scene, such as Japan and the newly-industrialising countries, the institutionalising of international economic cooperation is much more complex than it was during the period of US economic hegemony after World War II. The enormous growth in the scale and mobility of international capital flows has introduced a degree of volatility into the world economy that governments, even with maximum cooperation, will find difficult to control.

While no western country has escaped without a rise in unemployment, nevertheless the extent of the rise has varied considerably. In particular, there were a number of countries – notably Austria, Japan, Norway, Sweden and Switzerland – that continued to maintain low unemployment rates. Of special interest to Ireland is the fact that, with the exception of Japan, these were all small countries. An influential cross-country study some years ago (Therborn 1986) tried to identify what important relevant factors were shared in common by, and special to, this group of countries. The study concluded that the single most important common factor was the existence in all these countries of a long-standing social consensus to treat unemployment as an unacceptable feature of the economy. This strongly held consensus enabled them to develop policies and institutions, differing greatly from one country to the other, to preserve full employment even in a world of high unemployment.

THE IRISH CASE

Is the Irish case simply a reflection of the international forces we have been discussing? While accepting the pervasive impact of international developments on an economy as open as Ireland's, it is nevertheless necessary to recognise significant differences in the Irish case. First, and most important, is the fact that Ireland has always had a surplus labour problem: what is new is that more of this surplus is remaining in Ireland. Second, Ireland has had, and will continue for many years to have, a faster potential growth in its labour supply than other European countries. Furthermore, because of ease of migration, the Irish labour supply is more volatile than most, so that any attempt to bring down Irish unemployment through increased employment can be partly thwarted by reduced emigration or return flows from abroad. Third, given its small size and extreme openness, Keynesian demand policies were always of limited efficacy in addressing Ireland's development problems, and least of all when other countries had abandoned these policies: what really matters most is the enterprise and efficiency of the supply side of the economy, though of course the benefits accruing to a vibrant supply side will be greater the more buoyant the international economy. Fourth, while the popular view that unemployment is due to automation is not in accord with the facts in most countries, it cannot be ruled out in Ireland. An acceleration in technological progress would be expected to show up in higher productivity growth, whereas in fact productivity growth has fallen since 1973 in most OECD countries, but has risen substantially in Ireland[4] – as documented in Section 2.

A review of the chief studies seeking to explain the causes of Irish unemployment has been given in McGettigan (1992). The most sophisticated and systematic attempt is that of Barry and Bradley (1991), who used a disaggregated macroeconomic model to quantify the proximate causes of the rise in unemployment over the period 1970–87. They ascribed most of the changes in unemployment to three major influences (A) external factors, comprising changes in world demand, world interest rates and UK labour market conditions; (B) domestic policy, in terms of the supply-side and demand-side effects of fiscal policy; and (C) demographic factors, affecting labour supply. Over the full period 1970–87, the external factors accounted for nearly half of the total explained rise of ten percentage points, the demographic factors for about one-third, and domestic policy for only one-fifth. The impact of these forces, however, was quite different in the 1970s and 1980s. External factors were far more significant in raising unemployment in the 1980s than in the 1970s, while the reverse was true in the case of demographic factors. As regards domestic policy, it served to reduce unemployment in the 1970s but to raise it substantially in the 1980s. This does not mean, however, that fiscal policy was better in the first period. On the contrary, while it served to keep unemployment down temporarily this was only achieved by borrowing on a scale that gave rise to a huge build-up of national debt, and as pointed out already, made it impossible to avoid fiscal restraint in the later period.

Superficially, the Barry and Bradley results for the full period 1970–87 might suggest that the rise in Irish unemployment was largely due to factors beyond our control. A number of qualifications need to be applied, however, in drawing lessons from this type of causal analysis for policy purposes. First, the damage caused by the over-expansionary fiscal policy did not end with 1987. The huge debt which was built up has not even yet been brought fully under control: the continuing burden of servicing it and the retrenchment needed to reduce it still constrain the scope of policies that might be adopted to reduce unemployment. Second, while the net impact of domestic policy was found to be small over the full period studied, this does not mean that it would not be capable of a bigger, and better, impact. After all, domestic policy is something that one would hope could be used to reduce unemployment rather than add to it. If instead of a situation where domestic policy pushed up unemployment by two percentage points, we had been able to reverse that direction, then the implication is that unemployment could have been four percentage points lower – a not inconsiderable difference.

Finally, causal analyses typically assume that basic structures and institutions do not change in the period in question and therefore do not constitute causes. Thus, for example, if the wage bargaining mechanism results in wage cost competitiveness relative to other countries remaining unchanged during a given period, it will not emerge as a 'cause' of rising unemployment in that period. But simply maintaining competitiveness in an economy where the labour market has never cleared is not a very high aspiration. Moreover, this is something which is within control of domestic agents – though not necessarily within government control – whereas foreign demand is not. Consequently when conditions abroad deteriorate, one must be cautious about ascribing any consequential rise in unemployment solely to external factors: one might equally say in a more fundamental sense that the real cause is the failure of domestic agents to adjust internal structures in response to changes in the external environment.

The foregoing points lead to the important conclusion that, from a policy perspective, the prime interest lies in potential causes rather than historic causes. In other words, when considering ways of improving the unemployment situation, the causal forces that really matter are those which can not only affect unemployment but which are also potentially within our own control or influence – regardless of whether or not they have been established as causing past unemployment. In fact we know quite a lot about such potential causes – at least in regard to the direction, if not the exact size, of their potential impact. I shall argue later that our unwillingness to act derives less from lack of knowledge than from lack of will.

5. SCALE OF FUTURE CHALLENGE

The NESC (1991) report on emigration estimated the potential labour force increase in Ireland for each year up to 2006 on the assumption of no net emigration. What the exercise shows is that, due to the high birth rate up to 1980, the potential number of young entrants to the labour force remains high throughout the 1990s, but will fall thereafter. As a result, the potential increase in the labour force is in the region of 22–25,000 a year throughout the 1990s, but will fall rapidly to only 7,000 per annum by the middle of the next decade. The figures give some idea of the extraordinary high growth of employment that would be needed in the 1990s if Ireland were even to cater for new entrants to the labour force in a situation where there was no net emigration. If, in addition, there were to be a target of bringing down the level of unemployment by the year 2000 to the current EC level of about 10 per cent, this would require a further net addition of about 10,000 jobs a year. In round figures, the total required growth in employment to the end of the decade would be about 35,000 a year, or nearly 3 per cent per annum – way above anything ever achieved before.

These calculations do no more than give an idea of the scale of the challenge if Ireland were to cater fully for its potential labour force. As to what is actually likely to happen in practice, projections are made from time to time by the ESRI. The latest such projections up to the year 2000 were made before the international monetary crisis in September 1992, and assumed a moderate revival in the world economy beginning in the second half of that year. In such circumstances, the projections suggested that Ireland could attain an average GNP growth rate of 4 per cent per annum, which would generate an employment growth rate of 1 per cent per annum. Even with the expected renewal of emigration once the UK labour market recovered, unemployment in Ireland would still be slow to fall in this projection, and by the end of the decade would only be back to the level prevailing early in 1991, before the current recession.

Since this projection was prepared, the world economic outlook has deteriorated. The OECD has cut back its growth forecast for the industrialised world in 1993 to 1.9 per cent from a figure of 3 per cent forecast in June 1992. Of even more relevance to Ireland, the OECD has scaled down its forecast of European growth for 1993 from 2.4 to 1.2 per cent. Furthermore, no one can now be sure how long the current recession will last. Unemployment in the UK, which strongly influences Irish emigration, has risen more than anticipated and it is not clear when the rise will cease. In the light of these developments, the ESRI projection for Ireland given above must now be treated as too optimistic.

To what extent can we hope that national economic policy is geared to improving on this outlook? The most thorough and comprehensive recent attempt to define Irish economic policy is provided in the NESC (1990) report, *A Strategy for the Nineties*. This report classified the range of key policies needed for a consistent policy framework under three heads: macroeconomic policy designed to maximise the long-term growth potential of the economy; an income determination system to resolve distributional conflict in a peaceful way and to ensure improvement in competitiveness; and development policy to promote structural adjustment and encourage enterprise to take advantage of improved competitiveness and realise the growth potential. The NESC felt that while Ireland had in recent years put in place credible and consistent macroeconomic and incomes policies, this was not yet true in the case of development policy, a deficiency which the implementation of the Culliton Report (1992) could go some way to remedying. The NESC recognised, however, that during the nineties these policies would be unlikely to make much impact on unemployment, and that they should therefore be supported by

27

greatly enhanced manpower policies. The NESC accepted that such manpower policies would be costly, and stipulated that the funds would have to come from reductions in other areas of public expenditure. But public expenditure is already under severe pressure to make room for tax cuts and to meet the cost of high public sector pay increases. Furthermore, most other areas of public expenditure have been severely pruned in recent years, so that there is little possibility of securing further major cuts in existing programmes to transfer to manpower policies. There is no evidence of a willingness on the part of Irish society to reallocate resources to fund the 'radical approach to the problem of long-term unemployment', which the NESC held to be necessary.

If the foregoing assessment is a fair one, then only a dramatic improvement in Ireland's past performance and current prospective outlook would suffice to achieve a major impact on unemployment even ten years from now. In saying this, I am in no way denying that, notwithstanding some disastrous errors of policy, Irish performance over the past thirty years represents a considerable improvement on earlier history. In every five-year period since 1960, with the exception of 1980–85, the growth of real GNP has been in the region of 4 per cent per annum – a very respectable performance by international standards. The problem is that while this has been sufficient to reverse the previous long-term decline in employment, it has not yielded anything like enough employment growth to meet our needs. The challenge we face is whether we can further accelerate our rate of development, or restructure its pattern, in a way which does not involve the indefinite exclusion of a significant minority. That is a question that can be meaningfully addressed only in terms of long-term strategic options.

6. LONG-TERM STRATEGIC OPTIONS

In considering long-term strategic options, it is useful to keep an eye on whether there are any other countries which offer a model of what we might want to achieve. This is not to suggest that we can or should follow any such model blindly, but at the very least it is helpful to know that some other country in recent times has been capable of achieving what we might like to achieve. The range of options can be classified into four broad categories which, while by no means mutually exclusive, nevertheless in each case possess a distinct logic.

A. THE KOREAN MODEL

Let us first examine the most ambitious goal where Ireland would seek to generate employment growth at a rate that would eventually absorb its full labour force potential – both the unemployed and those who might otherwise emigrate – while at the same time raising its living standards towards the EC levels. That objective would require a high rate of growth of both employment and productivity, and this would only be possible with a much higher growth of output than we have experienced in the past for any sustained period: we would have to contemplate a rate of GNP growth of 6–7 per cent sustained over the next ten to fifteen years at least.

There is no model of such a performance in any western country over the past twenty years, nor is any in prospect over the next twenty years. To find a model of such a performance, it is necessary to look to a small group of newly industrialising countries, of which South Korea is a prime example – hence my designation of this as the Korean model. In the fifteen year period 1973–88, Korea achieved an average annual growth rate of GDP of 7.7 per cent, with an employment growth of 2.5 per cent per annum, and a productivity growth of 5 per cent. (Such rates imply a 50 per cent growth in employment over fifteen years and a doubling of product per worker.) That is the kind of performance which Ireland would have to attain to simultaneously achieve full employment while making strong progress in income convergence.

Such a performance would conceivably be within Ireland's compass if growth in the EC were as buoyant as it was in the postwar period up to 1973. Certainly, GNP growth rates approaching that level were achieved in the period 1960–73 by other low-income member states – Greece, Portugal and Spain – and there is no reason why Ireland could not now aim at a similar performance were Europe as a whole as buoyant as it was then. But there is strong theoretical and empirical support for the view that peripheral low-income countries find it very difficult to outpace the core, when the core areas are stagnant or declining (Kennedy 1992). It is not simply a question of the dampening impact of slow growth of demand in export markets: after all, Korea sells part of its output on these markets and has maintained high export growth through gaining market share. The more fundamental constraint is the degree to which Irish culture, attitudes, institutions etc. are bounded by European horizons. This makes any such performance implausible at a time of slow European growth – without a sea change in our whole philosophy and organisation of economic and social life of a kind that is difficult even to visualise.[5]

If this is so, then an essential pre-condition for substantially increasing the Irish growth rate is the resumption of buoyant growth in Europe; and the single most important issue for Ireland in Europe, therefore, is what EC macroeconomic policy will be in the years ahead. One of the concerns about economic and monetary union (EMU) in this regard is that, while it provides convincing institutional arrangements for community monetary policy, there is no fiscal authority of comparable weight, let alone an institutional counterpart responsible for the economic development of the

Community. And even though monetary policy will be centralised, there are fears that the balance may be weighted excessively towards price stability at the expense of employment and output. A continuation of a high level of real interest rates at a time when EC unemployment is not far below 10 per cent would be a major deterrent to reviving a buoyant European economy. Clearly, as a very small member state, Ireland has only a minimal role in influencing these issues, but it should continue to do what it can to keep the issues to the forefront of the Community's agenda, acting in concert with other like-minded member states.

B. THE AMERICAN MODEL

Another broad strategic option would be to try to achieve higher employment growth for any given output growth. The US offers an example of a country where even though output growth in the past thirty years has been less than in Ireland or in Europe, employment, chiefly in the market services sector, has consistently grown much faster. The corollary of course has been a much slower growth of productivity. Hence, this option would mean abandoning, for the time being at least, the goal of income convergence to European levels, though it could be argued that Ireland would be better placed to converge once the present enormous overhang of unemployment had been decisively reduced.

Raising the labour intensity of output in Ireland would involve concentrating on producing goods with a high labour content and/ or using techniques of production that involve high labour usage. In current circumstances there are severe limits on the degree to which this would be possible in the traded goods sector. The level of wages in Ireland is already at a height which makes it uneconomic to produce many traditional labour-intensive products. As a late-industrialising country there is much potential for catching up in productivity by importing technological improvements from abroad. Many of these technologies are labour saving, having been designed in richer countries at a time when labour was scarce (*see*, *for example* Romer 1987). Ireland depends heavily on foreign enterprise, and these companies tend to use standardised technological processes rather than altering techniques in response to local conditions. Attempts to raise labour intensity in the traded goods sector might have the undesirable consequence of lowering output growth.

The best hope of encouraging a radically greater degree of labour intensity in the market sector would be to try to create conditions in which low-wage services employment could flourish, and indeed a substantial proportion of the increased employment in the US takes that form. An inevitable corollary would be a slower growth in the pre-tax incomes of workers generally, a need for much wider gaps and greater flexibility in relative wages, and a reduction in welfare benefits – as is the case in the US. Real hourly earnings in the US as at August 1992 were nearly 5 per cent below the 1980 level, having remained fairly static up to 1986 but falling consistently since then. Furthermore the poverty rate in the US grew in the 1980s despite strong economic growth and even though employment among the poor rose. A recent study (Blank 1992) concluded that 'poverty increased during the 1980s because declines in the wages rates of the poor more than offset increases in their employment and days of work'.

The vast majority of the labour force in the US depends on there being an employer willing to offer a job, albeit sometimes at low wages: almost 90 per cent of the total work force are employees. There is no assurance that replication of US labour market conditions in a less highly developed country would produce a similar response from employers. The closest EC equivalent to US labour market conditions is probably Greece where the extremely limited coverage of unemployment compensation forces everyone to find some form of work, so that unemployment, however measured, is kept below the EC average. The resulting employment structure in Greece, however, is radically different from that of the US, or for that matter from Ireland. Only 50 per cent of those in civilian employment in Greece are employees (75 per cent in Ireland); 35 per cent of Greek workers are employers or self-employed (23 per cent in Ireland); and 14 per cent are classified as unpaid family workers (2 per cent in Ireland). Although these figures partly reflect the fact that agricultural employment remains more significant in Greece then in Ireland (27 per cent as against 15 per cent of total civilian employment), nevertheless even outside agriculture a similar disparity exists.

Whether such a society would represent an improvement on what we now have is very much a value judgement. Aside altogether from its desirability, there are severe constraints on its feasibility. Apart from the problem of gaining domestic political support for such an approach, and the fact that the trade union movement is vastly stronger in Ireland than in the US, this option could also be constrained by demonstration effects arising from membership of the EC. Ireland has had long experience of the degree to which its labour-market conditions have been affected by close institutional links and freedom of movement with a larger richer neighbour, the UK. Income expectations are influenced by the levels prevailing in the dominant partner and therefore tend to run ahead of domestic productivity. Consequential pressure for productivity growth to validate the higher incomes limits employment opportunities unless output growth is accelerated. If as a result of closer EC integration, the higher wage levels in the richer member states were to become part of the reference group in formulating domestic wage claims, then that would further constrain the scope for greater employment intensity. Moreover, the most likely consequence of a sharp curtailment of unemployment compensation in Ireland would be to force people to emigrate rather than enter into very low-wage activities at home, as in the US and Greece.

C. THE SCANDINAVIAN MODEL

The third option would be to increase the labour intensity of production, not in the market sector, but through publicly funded
activities. This approach would accept that productivity growth
would continue to be strong in the market sector in Ireland, but
would aim to siphon off part of the resulting income gain to finance
pro-active manpower policies, including employment in useful
public service and community activities. The jobs need not be
provided in the public sector as such, but could be sub-contracted
to private sector operators, but the bulk of the finance would have
to come from the public sector. The reason is that the activities
involved, however socially useful, do not arise from normal
market demand. In essence, the strategy seeks to curb the after-
tax incomes of the employed to provide the resources to give useful
work to those excluded from employment by market processes.

A strategy along these lines has long been followed in varying
degrees by the Scandinavian countries, and most notably by Sweden.
Sweden has refused to countenance the notion of long-term
unemployment and has been prepared to go to considerable
lengths to forestall and eliminate it through an active, integrated
set of manpower programmes. The Swedish approach combines
initial assessment and counselling of potentially vulnerable individuals, early training, measures to secure that jobs are available,
and a restrictive approach to paying unemployment benefit in
order to ensure cooperation in responding to these schemes.

The strategy is similar in fact to what the NESC (1990) report
had in mind when it called for a radically enhanced manpower
policy. In my view, however, the NESC did not fully face up to the
constraints on implementing such a strategy on the scale that would
be required in Ireland to bring down unemployment substantially.
First, putting the unemployed to work through active manpower
schemes costs more than paying unemployment compensation,

and for the reasons given in the previous section, it is hard to see how it could be accomplished without higher taxation. It is true that in Sweden the cost of their manpower measures as such is less than what Ireland pays in unemployment compensation, but that is because Sweden has managed to keep unemployment at a low level until recently, not only through manpower policy, but also through running a successful economy and maintaining a very large public service. Sweden is a country with exceptionally high tax levels.

Second, the challenge of organising effective work for the unemployed in public schemes would be enormous, given the scale of Irish unemployment. Sweden provides only a partial model in this regard because, given its persistent success over a long period in forestalling unemployment, the scale of the problem faced by its manpower programmes was never anything like what Ireland would now have to face. If the tasks involved were only of a 'make-work' variety, or if they were badly managed, then this would detract from, and discredit, the whole strategy.

Third, a major difficulty in organising useful work schemes for the unemployed in Ireland is trade union opposition to taking on unemployed workers at less than union rates of pay to do what is considered to be work appropriate to their members. This limits the kind of work that can be offered to low priority tasks. The unions would have no objection, of course, if the additional workers were taken on in the normal way, but the cost involved would then limit the numbers who could benefit. This problem is less acute in Sweden, not because trade unions there are any more tolerant of low-wage schemes, but rather for the paradoxical reason that since tax and unemployment compensation rates are so high, there is little extra exchequer cost in financing the re-employment of the unemployed at normal pay and conditions. Furthermore, trade union solidarity in Sweden is more effective in limiting pay increases in the public sector to those applying in the exposed sector.

Apart from the domestic constraints that would need to be ove-come, the strategy would also be constrained by closer European integration. Economic union inevitably creates competitive pressures forcing a certain degree of harmonisation in taxation. In addition, freedom of movement and measures designed to encourage political cohesion (such as the concept of European citizenship or the Social Charter) give rise to pressures to harmonise state benefits and services. In such circumstances a poorer member state could encounter increasing difficulties in balancing its budget, as is amply demonstrated by the historical experience of Northern Ireland in relation to the United Kingdom. But even a rich country would find it hard to sustain a high tax/high public services economy in a Community where the other members were moving in the opposite direction. Certainly Danish fears about the future of their 'Scandinavian model' in a closely integrated Europe was a major issue in their referendum campaign on the Maastricht Treaty. Furthermore, Sweden, which aspires to join the Community but is not yet a member, is now finding it increasingly difficult to sustain its strategy: in the last year its unemployment rate has risen to 5 per cent and threatens to rise further.

D. AN ENHANCED TRADITIONAL IRISH MODEL

A fourth option would be to embrace the full logic of freedom of movement within the EC so as to upgrade the traditional Irish way of coping with surplus labour by not only tolerating emigration but welcoming and encouraging a much higher level than has been experienced in the past twenty years or so. It could be argued that, with improvements in transport and communications, emigration no longer involves the traumatic lifetime separation which applied to traditional emigration, and that it would be much better for people to be employed abroad rather than unemployed at home. An obvious range of policy instruments could be adopted in pursuit of this strategy, such as enhanced placement services in relation to jobs abroad, upgrading of language and other skills etc. Other, less congenial, policy instruments could be employed, such as reducing the level or duration of unemployment benefits. The NESC (1991) report on emigration noted that during the 1980s the rewards from employment improved more rapidly in Britain than in Ireland, especially for those with above average earnings, partly because of tax changes, while, on the other hand, unemployment benefits improved more rapidly in Ireland, especially for the long-term unemployed. The report concludes that these trends 'suggest that those with high earnings potential will be particularly attracted by the prospects in Britain, whilst those who have been unemployed for some time or are likely to be employed at low incomes in Britain now have less incentive to emigrate'.

This strategy would mean abandoning the objective of trying to provide jobs at home for all who would prefer to work at prevailing wage levels in Ireland. While this might be no more than a recognition of the reality that Ireland has never before met that objective, and is unlikely to do so in the foreseeable future, the explicit adoption of this approach would give rise to many negative echoes from the past that would be seriously damaging to national morale. Moreover, it is also doubtful if the approach would enable Ireland ever to catch up with the rest of the EC in terms of living standards. Modern regional economic theory suggests that labour outflows at a rate involving a reduction in population may only reinforce the scale disadvantages of weaker areas (Krugman 1991). In his recent analysis of Ireland's long-term relative economic decline, Mjøset (1992) attributes a major role to emigration in accounting for the vicious circles he identified, and argues that only if emigration is stemmed can the supply of entrepreneurs be secured. Also, while traditionally in Ireland the bulk of the emigrants were among the least skilled, in recent times these have become relatively less mobile – so that substantially increased emigration could involve a major brain drain, while leaving behind a large substratum with low education and skills. Finally, Ireland would be embarking on such a strategy at a singularly unpropitious time in terms of conditions abroad, given the high and rising unemployment level in the UK and EC generally. It is impossible to say how long these conditions will last, but as long as they do they impose a severe constraint on the scope for this approach.

SUMMING-UP

While any one of the four options outlined above could be pursued in a variety of different ways, I am unaware of any approaches that are not encompassed in the four broad categories. The categories are not, in all respects, mutually exclusive, though any mix would of course require a compatible set of instruments that rule out other instruments. One could envisage, for instance, a coherent strategy that would put the main emphasis on faster growth (A), while encouraging somewhat greater labour intensity (B), coping with specially deprived labour market groups even at the cost of higher taxes (C), and recognising that for at least the next fifteen years or so, some emigration is inevitable (D). I have been at pains, however, to set out the chief constraints facing each strategy – not to induce despair but rather to demonstrate that very major changes in our economy and society would be required to attempt to pursue aggressively any one of these options, or any mix of them.

7. HOW TO MOTIVATE FUNDAMENTAL CHANGE

The question of how major changes are to be secured is one that has received insufficient attention in Ireland. The prevailing view is that the responsibility rests with the government, which is assumed to have the power to accomplish necessary changes – if only the government had the competence to identify, and the will to implement, the appropriate policies. That assumption runs deep at all levels of society in Ireland. It prevailed at the very foundation of the State: Meenan (1970) identified it as one of the major preconceptions about the economy at Independence. It has been fed ever since by successive governments, and is strongly held in practice by all social partners and interest groups. Even economists of the far right, with strongly held views about the power of the market, will, when confronted by a problem, instinctively respond by reference to what the government is expected to do about it.

While the role of government is pivotal, the limits of government action are too often ignored. A government, even with unlimited political power, cannot correct all forms of market failure, and particularly not the government of a very small country. Furthermore, the political power of a government is often severely constrained by the unwillingness of the electorate to support necessary remedies. The point has been well made recently by Kornai (1992) in regard to the regeneration of the Hungarian economy in the post-socialist phase:

> A wise and efficient government can accelerate this development, and governmental errors and omissions can impede it, but the final outcome of the transition is not in the government's hands. Under the new post-socialist system, the state can at most influence the economy. It cannot run the economy, which is propelled by the interests of those participating in it. This is one of the main advantages a market economy has over centrally managed socialism.

While these considerations apply to all democracies, the problem may be more acute in Ireland because of the catch-all nature of the two largest political parties. Breen et al. (1990) have argued that, as a result, successive governments have sought to placate all sectional interests, so that distributional issues are obfuscated rather than resolved: in short, in their view, 'the State has tended to give in rather than develop an overall strategy of development'. Nevertheless, the fact that Irish politics is so highly sensitive to voting reactions suggests that employment would be given a much higher priority by politicians if the electorate at large favoured this. The question then becomes one of how the electorate can be persuaded to accept radical changes which may not be in the short-term interests of a majority of them.

Appeals to patriotism or altruism seem to have very limited impact where bread and butter issues are concerned – except when the need becomes very acute, as in the case of famines, when the Irish people have shown themselves to be among the most generous in the world. Despite the fact that Ireland still remains an overwhelmingly Christian country, religious motivation has never been strong in regard to wider social responsibility. Notwithstanding the efforts of Church authorities over the past twenty years in producing a series of documents on Christian social responsibility, there is little evidence that the position so trenchantly criticised by Frank Duff (1966) has changed:

> Our Christianity is our chief boast in Ireland. But it is being understood and practised only in a partial sense, that is as an individualistic religion whereby one beautifies and saves one's own soul. It is not being practised as a social religion, i.e. as concerned with duty in every shape and form and exhibited towards one's fellowmen, individually and corporately. Without the practical living of the full Christian duty the theory is fruitless; without it we are thrown back on the caricature of Christianity.

The most recent pastoral of the Irish Episcopal Conference (1992), *Work is the Key*, seeks to counter the spirit of fatalism about unemployment, to show how every person can contribute to a solution, and to motivate the people to act in accordance with their moral responsibilities in the matter. If this message is to be effective, however, it must at least reach its intended audience, most of whom will not read the document. Much more thought needs to be given to mobilising all organs of the Church on an ongoing basis for this purpose.

Probably the most common way by which conditions for radical change in society are created is through shocks to the system. Mancur Olson (1982) in his book *The Rise and Decline of Nations* has identified numerous cases where a severe shock was instrumental in surmounting the inhibiting effect of established interest groups. At the present time, we are witnessing the radical changes taking place in the economies of East Europe and the Soviet Union following the collapse of centralised socialism.

Indeed it has been argued recently in the Irish case that in order 'to achieve a significant improvement in competitiveness it will be necessary to change the people in the Republic's labour force (e.g. by expanding awareness of external quality standards and best industrial practice)' and that 'the most likely means . . . is through some shock' (Hitchens and Birnie 1992). In practice, however, it is very rare for any government to deliberately engineer such a shock – for two obvious reasons. First, a government that is unable to effect change by more orderly measures is unlikely to be able to administer shocks. Second, there is no guarantee that shocks always stimulate a constructive response: they may in fact produce anarchy. For that reason most major shocks are not deliberately engineered, and one of the few which was – Mao's Cultural Revolution – is hardly a good model to follow.

The steep rise in unemployment might itself be expected to have constituted a major shock to the system: certainly, before it happened, everyone would have assumed that unemployment levels of 200,000 and upwards lasting for as long as a decade would have brought about radical changes. That it has not done so is partly a reflection of the characteristics of the unemployed, discussed in Section 3, which make it difficult to organise them as a coherent political force. The majority of the population are not directly affected, do not fully appreciate the corrosive long-term consequences for the whole society, and therefore balk at the transformation that would be needed to do anything really substantial about the problem. Many would not gain, at least in the short term, from reducing unemployment, and the existence of polarised groups in society can impede necessary reforms (Alesina and Drazen 1991). Perhaps most of all there is the underlying hope that emigration will come to the rescue again, so as to contain unemployment until such time as the potential labour inflow falls as a result of the decline in the birth rate.

The real evil of emigration was that it enabled Ireland to avoid facing up to its responsibilities in the way other countries have been forced to do. It is worth noting that there is a close parallel here with the abortion issue. For an Irish pro-life person the really substantive issue should surely be how to minimise the number of Irish women having abortions. Yet, because of the ease of travel to Britain for abortion, the focus of attention is overwhelmingly on limiting the number taking place on Irish territory. Were it impossible for Irish women to go to Britain for abortion, we would then as a nation have to confront the full reality of the problem. The limited value of legal prohibition on its own would become apparent, and the efforts of those of us opposed to abortion would have to concentrate much more on addressing the conditions which each year precipitate 4,000 Irish women into choosing that option. Equally, legislators would face the choice of legislating for abortion or risk the development of widespread illegal abortion. The fact that we are saved from such unpleasant choices is convenient but does not make our society morally superior to others. Similarly, while emigration has been a convenient way of getting rid of surplus labour, the end result is not a more vibrant economy than elsewhere.

Nevertheless, the high level of unemployment has generated wide concern which is likely to be sustained at least as long as the emigration option is curtailed. It is vital now to capitalise on this concern and utilise it constructively to generate a sense of national purpose. In particular, it is very important to encourage debate among the public at large about the longer-term options open to us, and the often painful choices that need to be made *now* as well as in the future, if we were to pursue any chosen strategy effectively.

A further daunting factor inhibiting change is the lack of conviction that any solution can be found. Irish people are well aware that throughout the western world there is no longer a consensus about how to attain full employment, or indeed if it can be attained at all; and they doubt whether Ireland can succeed where so many other countries have failed. It is understandable that people will shrink from addressing a problem if they believe it to be insoluble. This leads to a chicken-and-egg situation where people will not face the problem because it is so difficult, while they have no hope whatever of overcoming the difficulties unless they face up to the problem.

As I have been at some pains to demonstrate, however, the Irish situation differs in important respects from that of other western countries. It is in the large part a long-standing problem of underdevelopment. True, we could tackle it more effectively if other countries were more buoyant, but it will not go away even if other countries solve *their* unemployment problem. It is a problem we ourselves must solve unless we are content to remain a back-water of Europe. Furthermore, even in a static world economy, a small country has an advantage in that it can still find adequate markets abroad if it is sufficiently innovative and flexible.

It was considerations such as the foregoing which led many groups and individuals to support the idea of a National Forum on Unemployment. Integral to that proposal was the idea that, like the New Ireland Forum, public sessions would be held under an independent chair at which all political parties, social partners, economists etc. would be called on to present their proposals in regard to unemployment and would be subject to cross examination on what these proposals might yield. At the very least this process would force all concerned to address the totality of the problem in a realistic way: at present there is a general reluctance to confront the full scale of the problem and most proposals touch only on the margins of it. As such the process could have a profound effect on popular opinion, generating a widespread impatience with vested interests so as to enable any government to act more decisively.

While the idea of a Forum on Unemployment received wide support, there was less agreement in regard to the role of such a body or how it should be constituted. Since the idea drew its inspiration from the New Ireland Forum, it is worth recalling some of the key features which probably contributed to its success. The New Ireland Forum was established

> for consultations on the manner in which lasting peace and stability could be achieved in a new Ireland through the democratic process and to report on possible new structures and processes through which this objective might be achieved (New Ireland Forum 1984).

At its first public session on 30 May 1983, the then Taoiseach, Dr Garret FitzGerald, stated his reason for initiating the Forum as follows:

> It was because of my conviction that we, the people of
> this state, have not sufficiently stirred outselved to face
> reality, that I proposed the establishment of this Forum.

The Forum was intended as a once-off enterprise, and in practice completed its business within about one year. An impressive measure of pre-planning was undertaken however, before the Forum was set up at all. The leaders of the four participating parties met on 14 and 21 April 1983 to consider the arrangements. They jointly selected an independent chairperson, and these five formed a Steering Geroup which subsequently met together on no less than 56 occasions, or approsimately once a week during the lifetime of the Forum. The 27 members of the Forum itself were all top politicians, including the four party leaders. They were serviced by a high-level independent secretariat, the Secretary being the Clerk of Seanad Éireann and the co-ordinator of the team being an Assistant Secretary in the Taoiseach's Office. The Forum held 28 private sessions and 13 public sessions, which were widely reported. It invited oral presentations from 31 individuals and groups and considered 317 written submissions.

This huge commitment on the part of so many important and busy people was proportionate to the scale and urgency of the task in hand. I believe that the same high level of commitment would be helpful now in getting the Irish people to 'face reality' in regard to the efforts needed to tackle the unemployment crisis. Both the Oireachtas Committee on Employment, set up by the last government, and the National Economic and Social Forum, proposed by the present government, fall far short of this level of commitment and have failed to capture the popular imagination. A Forum on Unemployment more akin to the New Ireland Forum would be better placed to mobilise and harness public concern for creative purposes.

8. POLICY PRINCIPLES

The exact meaning of the word crisis, used in the title of this paper, is 'a time for decisive change'. While many people apply the term to the current unemployment situation, there is little evidence that they are using it in its exact sense. Nevertheless concern about unemployment is giving rise to a greater questioning of vested interests, and a mood for at least modest change. That incremental reforms are unlikely to be capable of dealing with the totality of the problem is no reason for not carrying them through. We must begin somewhere, and it is better to secure modest progress than no progress at all. Furthermore even modest success would boost confidence to a degree that might generate support for more substantial approaches. A variety of policy proposals has been put forward from various sources in the past year (*see, in particular*, the various papers in Gray 1992, Keane 1993, and Studies 1993). It is not possible here in a short pamphlet to examine these proposals in detail. Instead I confine myself to drawing attention to some key issues of principle within the kind of policy framework that is likely to be feasible in Ireland in the years ahead.

THE ECONOMIC ENVIRONMENT

This currency crisis which began in September 1992 made clear that, though there was strong verbal support for the hard currency stance, there was insufficient appreciation of the disciplines needed to sustain it. The advantages of a hard currency stance can only be gained if these disciplines are understood and respected. The hard currency option promises an environment of low inflation and, in normal circumstances, lower interest rates than would otherwise prevail. This represents an important contribution to potential employment expansion and a solid basis for developing appropriate long-term strategies. In order to defend the hard currency, however, monetary policy must be dedicated to protecting the exchange rate. Moreover, if interest rates are to be kept at moderate levels, fiscal restraint is also necessary – especially given the need to reduce the still very high debt level. For the defence and expansion of employment, the wage bargaining system now takes centre stage: this system must be geared to improving competitiveness over the longer term, while in the short term it must be capable of reacting flexibly to external shocks. Furthermore, responsibility for taking advantage of the stable monetary environment and improved competitiveness devolves mainly on the enterprise sector without recourse to major hand-outs which would jeopardise the government's fiscal position.

This strategy has much to recommend it for a small, highly open economy, and indeed has been followed successfully by Austria since World War II. The preconditions for success as outlined in the previous paragraph have not been communicated effectively, however. During the currency crisis that began in Autumn 1992, when the hard currency strategy was under severe pressure, various proposals were made to alleviate the position of exporters to the UK. Many of these proposals would have placed an added burden on the exchequer, when what was needed to sustain confidence in the currency was a strengthening of the fiscal position. Only a few voices called for a re-negotiation of the PESP, which had been negotiated at a time when prices were expected to rise more than would happen with a strengthening of the Irish pound; while the most appropriate means of financing any exchequer subsidy to the exposed sector would have been by deferring or cancelling special pay increases in the public service.

Given that the necessary domestic adjustments were not made, and made decisively, speculation against the Irish pound continued and in the end, forced a devaluation. Nevertheless, the preservation of the new Irish ERM parity remains the best basis for long-term strategy, and hopefully some useful lessons for the future will have been learned from the currency crisis. There are indications already that the jobs/income trade-off is now more fully adverted to in the exposed sector, but it is not at all clear that the message has yet reached the sheltered sector, of which the public service is a large part. The public service is in a unique position in that most of its members are not liable to unemployment. When in the 1980s a voluntary redundancy scheme was introduced to cut public service numbers, it was given on terms far more favourable than any private sector employer could afford. Moreover, public service workers do not pay the unemployment component of PRSI on the grounds that, since they are not liable to unemployment, they cannot benefit. Their security from unemployment, however, is not divinely ordained: rather it is a privilege accorded by the taxpayer which puts them in a more favourable position than most other workers, and as such should require a larger contribution, rather than no contribution at all. If, for example, the Voluntary Health Insurance (VHI) could offer two policies, one with cover for medical expenses and the other guaranteeing perfect health, then no one would object to paying more for the latter! The arrangements for pay determination in the public service require to be reviewed urgently in the light of these considerations. The same applies to fee income paid from the exchequer to professionals (e.g. doctors, lawyers etc.) who are not employees. In the private sector, the Single European Market may help to curb the practice in some Irish companies of awarding executives huge levels of remuneration (including stock options etc.) even when the companies they managed were in difficulties.

The need for a vibrant indigenous manufacturing and traded goods sector was a dominant theme in the Culliton report, and unless there is an adequate entrepreneurial response, no amount of government activity can substitute. Nevertheless there are important ways in which a government can set an environment favourable to economic enterprise, apart from its role in sustaining a stable macroeconomic framework. The key areas are (i) infrastructure, (ii) the incentive/disincentive effects of taxation and public expenditure, and (iii) the moderation of restrictive practices.

Infrastructure takes in both the physical infrastructure (notably transport, communications and energy) and the general level and quality of human resources (education and training). A good deal of progress has already been made, and is being made, on these fronts, and the EC Structural Funds have been valuable in providing additional funding for such development. But in a number of cases it is not just extra funding that is needed but the tackling of institutional rigidities. For example, in a country which is prone to emphasising its peripherality, we are shooting ourselves in the foot by the way we have managed, or mismanaged, our major port in Dublin. The Culliton recommendations on this and other infrastructural factors, if implemented, should prove helpful.

As regards the incentive/disincentive impact of taxation, undue attention has focused on the overall level of taxation. The reality is that, in Irish circumstances, no great reduction in overall taxation levels can realistically be expected: on the contrary the general level of taxation would have to rise if we were to take extensive manpower measures in relation to the unemployed. The general level of taxation is not as big a disadvantage as is often claimed: countries have managed to operate efficiently at widely different tax/GNP ratios. What is more important than the overall level is how the incentive structure of taxation is geared towards the attainment of the needs of society, and how effectively the tax revenue is spent.

In this context, it may be noted that in Ireland taxation is always regarded as a disincentive. This in fact is not the case: taxes can also be used as incentives to achieve social goals. The following example, deliberately chosen from the US, will illustrate the point, though it is not suggested that Ireland ought to follow this particular example. In some states of the US, firms with high lay-offs have to pay higher taxes to cover the extra costs of the unemployment benefits drawn by their employees. This practice is technically known as 'experience rating', and the rationale is that, without complete experience rating, the firms with low lay-offs would be subsidising those with high lay-offs. A recent study of the practice (Card and Levine 1992) estimated that its extension to all states in the US would lower the national unemployment rate by about one percentage point in the trough of a recession. In Ireland, one can visualise how such a system would be attacked as forcing firms to keep on workers they do not need, whereas it is used in the US as an efficient way of inducing firms to weigh the private benefit to them of laying off workers against the wider social costs of their actions.

More generally in regard to the incentive/disincentive effects of public spending and taxation, a distinction needs to be drawn between an absolute incentive to a given activity or behaviour and a relative incentive to it compared with other activities or behaviours. The snag with absolute incentives is that they are costly to the exchequer – a major consideration given the pressure on the public finances. But it is possible to improve relative incentives without any net cost to the exchequer. For example, if we wish to favour manufacturing over other types of enterprise, then instead of giving yet another tax break to manufacturing, its relative attractiveness could be improved by removing tax breaks in other sectors, or imposing taxes on them.

This approach has been under-utilised in Ireland. Indeed, the opposite is what has tended to happen. A tax incentive is given to encourage manufacturing, such as the 10 per cent corporation tax rate, but its impact in improving the relative attractiveness of manufacturing investment is later diluted by such measures as Section 23 relief for construction. The end result is that the exchequer is left to carry a heavy cost, while the aim of improving the attractiveness of investment in manufacturing relative to property is negated. Previous research has identified a whole plethora of such tax incentives to investment in housing, other property and financial assets. These are activities which the Irish have not been slow to enter, whereas the record of indigenous industry shows the considerable difficulties involved there. A decisive approach needs to be taken to reducing the range of tax and other incentives applying to 'rent-seeking' activities, which encourage redistribution of wealth rather than its creation. These are probably much more significant than the labour market disincentives arising from the tax and social welfare systems, which have attracted much greater attention. Nevertheless, a great deal of remedial disincentives affecting the labour market have been identified which should be systematically removed.

Measures to encourage competition and break down restrictive practices in professions (such as law, accounting, medicine, auctioneering, stockbroking etc.) and in financial services have an obvious role in increasing efficiency and opening up employment opportunities. Likewise, Gray (1992) has drawn attention to the fact that government regulation of various services (e.g. taxi-drivers and publicans) may restrict entry and limit employment opportunities. If these are tackled piecemeal, it will be interpreted as a selective attack on each particular group. To have any hope of success there would need to be an across the board review of state restrictions which unnecessarily limit employment opportunities – to be done in the context of a more wide-ranging attack on restrictive practices by private interest groups.

There is nothing to be gained from making excessive claims for the benefits of any one of the tax reforms or other measures outlined above, or indeed for the package as a whole. In this connection it is salutary to note that recent studies of the impact of the major tax reduction and tax reform programmes implemented by President Reagan in the US during the 1980s – involving a cut in the top marginal rate from 70 per cent to 28 per cent – have found that the response was 'much smaller than ardent supply-side revolutionaries expected' (Slemrod 1992). The evidence suggests a hierarchy of responses, at the top of which is the timing of economic transactions, followed by financial and accounting responses, but 'at the bottom of the hierarchy, where the least response is evident, are the real decisions of individuals and firms' (ibid.). Similarly, in the United Kingdom the radical attacks by the Thatcher government on restrictive practices in industrial relations have not precluded unemployment from rising rapidly again. Nevertheless, there is no excuse for the government maintaining disincentives to the achievement of broadly agreed social goals. While no one change on its own will produce dramatic results, the sum total of such measures could in time yield significant benefits.

ECONOMIC ENTERPRISE

Given the past history of Irish business enterprise, however, it is hard to be confident that a favourable environment will suffice without also seeking innovative methods to elicit and develop more enterprise. Indigenous industry has so far resisted the most vigorous efforts of industrial policy to bring about its development. The Culliton report itself, while placing the main emphasis on environmental factors, was not confident that this would be enough, and recommended the continuance of a reformed industrial policy. Its concrete recommendations in relation to indigenous industry are weak, however: the proposal for a new agency is problematic, while the implications of replacing grants with equity have not been thought through. No one can yet claim to have discovered the formula for energising indigenous private industry.

It would therefore be foolish to overlook any potential means of mobilising alternative sources of economic enterprise. Hence the potential of state enterprises should not be curtailed by ideological inhibitions or by recent alleged scandals in a few of them. If they are to function satisfactorily, however, public enterprises must be allowed to operate in a framework free from arbitrary political interference, be given clearly-defined commercial objectives and be held fully accountable for the results. This would need to be underpinned by a well-informed public opinion with an acceptance of the fact that a viable public enterprise sector is incompatible with subsidising lame ducks indefinitely. A possible way of implementing this approach would be the establishment of an overall state holding company as a source of risk capital for new ventures by individual state companies with a capacity for diversification and growth.[6]

A feature of Irish attempts to promote industrial development is the degree to which this function is seen as solely a state responsibility. It is true that the representative associations for industry and its component sectors do carry out some developmental functions on behalf of members, but these are small compared with the emphasis on lobbying activities. This is not true to the same extent in many other more successful countries. In Finland, for example, firms have at their disposal a wide array of support from private organisations and associations in matters such as export development, technology acquisition and training. Some of the bodies are funded totally by members while others receive some form of state subvention. The key role played by industrial associations in Germany, Japan and Switzerland in relation to the creation and dissemination of information on product development, technology and marketing, and the organisation of training, has been emphasised by Grubel (1993). Programmes organised and paid for by members of private sector associations would be likely to keep a close watch on achieving value for money. There may be a case for providing a subvention for a limited period to match members' contributions for programmes worked out with the Department of Enterprise and Employment or with the state agencies. Such subventions should have a definite termination date after which, once the benefits of the programmes were clear to member firms, they would be financed entirely from the private sector. Similarly, there is need to get private firms to appreciate the value of training, and to wean them from almost exclusive dependence on the state for something that they should be paying for themselves.

What about trade unions and enterprise? In an address to the ICTU Annual Summer Course in 1977 (Kennedy 1977), I made the following proposal to the assembled delegates:

> And might I also draw to your attention, hopefully for your consideration during this course, that trade union enterprise has been a major source of development in Israel. Apart from its many affiliated co-operatives, the trade union movement there developed large industrial enterprises accounting for nearly 20% of the nation's industrial value adding and embracing such industries as metals, chemicals, electronics and construction. In addition, the trade union movement operates one of the largest banks (with over 200 branches) and has a virtual monopoly of bus transport. The basic motivation underlying such enterprise was to help provide jobs directly for the people rather than leaving the task solely to the government and private industry. If, as trade unionists, you believe that the task is one for the State, then I might ask you to consider why you expect the State to be more enterprising than the people forming it, of whom trade union members represent a very considerable portion.

I may add that when the delegates returned from the workshops at which they considered my address, of all the unpalatable proposals I had made to them, including the need for pay restraint, none attracted more vehement antipathy and outright incredulity than the idea of trade union enterprise! But the level of unemployment then, though considered at the time quite unacceptable, was only one-third of the present level – so perhaps the idea is deserving of renewed consideration by trade unionists.

One hopeful sign in Ireland is that at local community level there is some evidence of a flowering of community enterprise. This has been given less notice than it deserves. The assessment by O'Malley (1992) of the Pilot Programme for Integrated Rural Development received virtually no attention from the national media, even though it demonstrated that it is possible, at little expense to the taxpayer, to stimulate considerable voluntary effort by local people to promote economic and social development in their own areas. Interesting initiatives have also been taken at local level in the implementation of various manpower schemes, and in organising self-help among the unemployed. The goodwill is there: what is often missing is the means of mobilising it and managing it effectively. This is an area where a voluntary contribution from private business in the form of secondment of professional business management could be very valuable.

THE STATE AS EMPLOYER OF LAST RESORT?

It would be dishonest not to admit that however successfully the foregoing policy principles were applied, large numbers would still remain unemployed throughout the next ten years or more, many of whom would be long-term unemployed. The state has already assumed financial responsibility for their support, but the situation can hardly be regarded as satisfactory for society at large, and least of all for the unemployed themselves. The unemployment compensation system was designed originally to cushion temporary spells of unemployment and not to deal with unemployment of unlimited duration. Even if the state had the means to do so, it is effectively precluded from providing an adequate income for the long-term unemployed by virtue of the need to preserve the incentive to work. Moreover, as William Beveridge put it, 'complete idleness even on an income demoralises'.

The chief alternative open to the state would be to provide, or to fund the provision of, work for those unemployed beyond a certain period (say one year). This could be accompanied where necessary by relevant training, but training without the assurance of related work has little to recommend it for the long-term unemployed. There is no shortage of socially useful work to be done, though its effective organisation would be challenging. The greater problem, however, is how to pay for it: it costs more than unemployment compensation and therefore requires higher taxes (not borrowing!). This could have some negative effects on employment in the rest of the economy, but these effects would be small *provided* the rest of the community were willing to bear the increased taxes without demanding compensation through higher wages etc. It is resistance to the real income cut that constitutes the ultimate barrier.

The successful operation of this approach would require a public opinion imbued by the philosophy expressed in the title of an interesting book on economic policy by an American economist, *Hard Heads, Soft Hearts* (Blinder 1987). We would need to be soft-hearted in our willingness to share income, but hard-headed in our insistence both that the work would be effectively organised and that the long-term unemployed would be expected to accept any such work which broadly conformed to their skills or qualifications.

9. CONCLUSION

It is not at all clear that Irish society is ready to accept the kind of changes needed to address the unemployment crisis. Jean Monnet (1978) remarked in his memoirs that 'people only accept change when they are faced with necessity, and only recognise necessity when a crisis is upon them'. Many people in Ireland now agree that the unemployment situation constitutes a crisis, but there is little disposition to tackle it as such: it remains for too many only a verbal crisis, analogous to verbal Republicanism of former times.

In this pamphlet, I have tried above all to show that unemployment is a responsibility of the whole community. It is not a problem that any government can tackle effectively unless the community in general is willing to accept large and often unpalatable changes. It is certainly not one for which experts can offer a ready-made solution: what they can usefully do is help in conceptualising the issues and point to options which could improve matters, while being frank about the costs attached to each. In the end of the day, however, the pursuit of any option depends on the choices that society is willing to make, or at least tolerate. Ideas need the support of ideals.

No problem can be solved unless it is confronted by those with the power to do something about it. The brunt of unemployment is borne by those with little power, while those with power have for long been unwilling to confront the problem. Scarcity of jobs is not new in Ireland and has been accepted with complacency in the past because of the safety valve of emigration. Now that this escape route has been closed off, at least temporarily, there is an historic opportunity to build a national consensus to address the problem meaningfully and to accept the changes which would be entailed.

A realistic approach must recognise that, while we have to begin now, the effort will need to be sustained over a long period. Consequently, it will require a much greater degree of strategic thinking and planning than we have been accustomed to in the past. It will also call for greater self assurance in exercising our role in the EC – not only in taking full advantage of opportunities already available but also in seeking to influence EC policy to complement our own efforts.

NOTES

1 The measurement of unemployment is not an exact science. There is agreement that for purposes of international comparison an unemployed person should be defined as one who is without gainful employment, available for work, and actively seeking work. The application of these criteria is by no means straightforward and different sources yield different estimates. The most widely known source in Ireland is the Live Register (LR) count available at the end of each month. Since the count reflects the administrative rules applying to registration, it is not an ideal measure of the level of unemployment. Some people who are undoubtedly unemployed may not satisfy the registration rules, while others who do may not really be unemployed in the sense defined above. Changes in the rules may also affect the LR as an indicator of trends over time, while differences between countries make it inappropriate for international comparisons. The other main source of unemployment data is the annual Labour Force Survey (LFS), based in Ireland on a sample of about 45,000 households and conducted simultaneously throughout the EC. Two measures of unemployment are commonly drawn from the LFS. The first estimate, known as Principal Economic Status (PES), relies on the respondents' own assessment of their usual situation in regard to employment and unemployment. These responses can be processed quickly to yield early results, but suffer from a degree of subjectivity in how respondents classify themselves. The second estimate, based on guidelines by the International Labour Office (ILO), analyses the respondents' answers to a range of questions in the LFS about their actual situation in the week before the survey. This is the preferred method of measurement, especially for international comparisons, but only becomes available following a full analysis of the survey results. The PES and ILO measures yield roughly similar estimates of the total numbers unemployed, but differ significantly on some of the components. The LR measure yields a significantly higher estimate of total unemployment in recent years: in April 1992, when the LFS–PES total was 225,000, the LR figure

was 281,000. It should be noted, however, that far from being unique, the gap between the registered and LFS measures of total unemployment is similar in Ireland to that of several other EC member states, including Germany. While the differences in measurement are important, they should not deflect attention from the more important fact that unemployment, however measured, has reached a shockingly high level in Ireland.

2 The numbers on the Live Register fell by only 7,000 from 1985 to 1990. A large proportion of the difference arises from the fact that whereas the LFS estimates of female unemployment show a fall of about 13,000, the numbers registered as unemployed rose by 12,000. This disparity partly reflects the easing of registration rules: the Social Welfare (No. 2) Act 1985 removed restrictions on married women in particular signing on the register. Another important reason for the different overall trends in the LFS and LR measures in this period was high emigration of young people who would be classified as unemployed on the LFS basis but would not qualify for inclusion on the LR.

3 Of course, to the extent that the higher proportion of adults not in gainful employment in Ireland provides a relatively greater volume of household services than in Denmark, it could be argued that Ireland's true relative income per capita is understated. This point raises difficult conceptual and measurement problems which are not addressed adequately in conventional national income statistics. For a pioneering exploratory examination of the issues involved, see Fahey (1992)

4 While Irish productivity growth has been artificially inflated to a significant but unknown degree by transfer pricing on the part of foreign multinationals, it is unlikely that this alone could account for the acceleration. On the general issue of the relation between productivity growth and unemployment, Aghion and Howitt (1992) make the case that technological innovations, by creating a need for a faster rate of worker retraining in order to use the new technologies, can lead to a permanently higher rate of unemployment.

5 A key element in the success of Korea and the other rapidly-growing countries of South-East Asia, which would be difficult to replicate in Ireland, has been their extraordinary flexibility and speed of adjustment to changing world market and product conditions. For example, Korean exports to Saudi Arabia rose 37-fold from 1973 to 1977. Later, when the US market was particularly buoyant from 1980 to 1985, the share of Korean exports going to the US rose from 26 to 36 per cent. Korean exports of ships, which accounted for only 4 per cent of its total exports in 1980, had risen to 17 per cent by 1985 (Dervis and Petrie 1987). The same amazing ability to adapt the product range is found at company level. The World Bank (1987) study cites as typical the case of the Handok Company, employing 3,500 workers: in 1971, 95 per cent of its sales were human-hair wigs; by 1976, paper was the largest contributor to sales; by 1981, watches constituted 85 per cent of sales; and by 1985, while watches were still a major component (at 45 per cent), they were now rivalled by computer sales (at 41 per cent). It would be quite wrong to conclude, however, that Korea's development happened purely through the unaided operation of market forces: as well, 'government played a central role through its pervasive control of the financial sector as well as trade policy and other instruments'. (Dervis and Petrie 1987)

6 These and other aspects of developing a vibrant state enterprise sector are examined in Sweeney (1990).

BIBLIOGRAPHY

Aghion, P. and P. Howitt (1992) "Unemployment and growth through creative destruction", mimeo.

Alesina, A. and A. Drazen (1991) "Why are stabilizations delayed?", *American Economic Review*, Vol. 81, No. 5, December

Barry, F. and J. Bradley (1991) "On the causes of Ireland's unemployment", *Economic and Social Review*, Vol. 22, No. 4, July

Blank, R. (1992) *Why were Poverty Rates so High in the 1980s?*, NBER Working Paper No. 3878

Blinder, A. S. (1987) *Hard Heads, Soft Hearts: Tough-minded Economics for a Just Society*, Reading, Mass.: Addison-Wesley

Breen, R., D. Hannan, D. Rottman and C. Whelan (1990) *Understanding Contemporary Ireland: State, Class and Development in the Republic of Ireland*, Dublin: Gill and Macmillan

Breen, R. (1991) *Education, Employment and Training in the Youth Labour Market*, General Research Series No. 152, Dublin: ESRI

Callan, T., B. Nolan and B. J. Whelan, D. F. Hannan with S. Creighton (1989) *Poverty, Income and Welfare in Ireland*, General Research Series No. 146, Dublin: ESRI

Card, D. and P. Levine, (1992) *Unemployment Insurance Taxes and the Cyclical and Seasonal Properties of Unemployment*, NBER Working Paper No. 4030

Culliton, J. (1992) (Chairman) *A Time for Change: Industrial Policy in the 1990s*, Report of the Industrial Policy Review Group, Dublin: Stationery Office

Dervis, K. and P. A. Petrie (1987) "The macroeconomics of successful development: What are the lessons?" in S. Fischer (ed.) *NBER Macroeconomics Annual 1987*, Cambridge, Mass: MIT Press

Duff, F. (1966) *True Devotion to the Nation*, Dundalk: Dundalgan Press

Fahey, T. (1992) "Housework, the household economy and economic development in Ireland since the 1920s", *Irish Journal of Sociology*, Vol. 2

Gray, A. W. (1992) "Expanding employment – the need for improved policy responses" in A. W. Gray (ed.) *Responses to Irish Unemployment*, Dublin: Indecon

Grubel, H. G. (1993) "Doubts about the new growth theory", *Swiss Review of World Affairs*, February

Hitchens, D. M. W. N. and J. E. Birnie (1992) "The competitive performance of the Republic of Ireland: a case of the British disease?" read at Statistical and Social Inquiry Society of Ireland Symposium on "Findings of the Industrial Policy Review Group", March 26

Irish Episcopal Conference (1992) *Work is the Key: Towards an Economy that Needs Everyone*, Dublin: Veritas

Keane, C. (ed.) (1993) *The Jobs Crisis*, The Thomas Davis Lecture Series, Cork and Dublin: Mercier Press (in association with RTE)

Kennedy, K. A. (1977) "Job creation since the foundation of the State" in *Industrial Development and Job Creation*, Dublin: Irish Congress of Trade Unions

Kennedy, K. A., T. Giblin and D. McHugh (1988) *The Economic Development of Ireland in the Twentieth Century*, London: Routledge

Kennedy, K. A. (1992) "Real convergence, the European Community and Ireland", Presidential Address to the Statistical and Social Inquiry Society of Ireland, May

Kornai, J. (1992) "The postsocialist transition and the state: reflections in the light of Hungarian fiscal problems", *American Economic Review*, Vol. 82, No. 2, May

Krugman, P. (1991) "Increasing returns and economic geography", *Journal of Political Economy*, Vol. 99, No. 3, June, pp. 483–499

Layard, R., S. Nickell and R. Jackman (1991) *Unemployment: Macroeconomic Performance and the Labour Market*, Oxford and New York: Oxford University Press

Lee, J. J. (1989) *Ireland 1912–1985. Politics and Society*, Cambridge University Press

McGettigan, D. (1992) "Irish unemployment: A review of the issues", Central Bank of Ireland: Technical Paper 2/RT/92

Meenan, J. F. (1970) *The Irish Economy Since 1922*, Liverpool University Press

Mjøset, L. (1992) *The Irish Economy in a Comparative Institutional Perspective*, NESC Report No. 93, Dublin: Stationery Office

Monnet, J. (1978) *Memoirs*, New York: Doubleday

BIBLIOGRAPHY

National Economic and Social Council (1990) *A Strategy for the Nineties*, Report No. 88, Dublin: NESC

National Economic and Social Council (1991) *The Economic and Social Implications of Emigration*, Report No. 90, Dublin: NESC

New Ireland Forum (1984) *Report*, Dublin: Stationery Office, May.

O'Donnell, R. (1992) "Economics and policy: Beyond science and ideology", *Economic and Social Review*, Vol. 24, No. 1, October

Olson, M. (1982) *The Rise and Decline of Nations*, Yale University Press

O'Malley, E. (1992) *The Pilot Programme for Integrated Rural Development 1988–90*, Broadsheet Series No. 27, Dublin: ESRI

Phelps, E. S. (1992) "A review of *Unemployment*", *Journal of Economic Literature*, Vol. 30, No. 3, September

Romer, P. M. (1987) "Crazy explanations for the productivity slowdown" in S. Fischer (ed.) *NBER Macroeconomics Annual 1987*, Cambridge, Mass: MIT Press

Slemrod, J. (1992) "Do taxes matter? Lessons from the 1980s", *American Economic Review*, Vol. 82, No. 2, May

Studies (1993) *Unemployment in the Republic of Ireland*, contributions by various authors, *Studies*, Vol. 82, No. 325, Spring

Sweeney, P. (1990) *The Politics of Public Enterprise and Privatisation*, Dublin: Tomar

Therborn, G. (1986) *Why Some People are more Unemployed than Others*, London: Verso

Whelan, C. T. and D. F. Hannan, S. Creighton (1991) *Unemployment, Poverty and Psychological Distress*, General Research Series No. 150, Dublin: ESRI

World Bank (1987) *Korea: Managing the Industrial Transition*, Washington, DC: World Bank

Wrigley, L (1985) "Ireland in economic space" in J. J. Lee (ed.) *Ireland: Towards a Sense of Place*, Cork University Press